CITIZENSHIP

A MANUAL *for* VOTERS

by
Emma Guy Cromwell

Lire Books : New York

Citizenship: A Manual for Voters

Copyright © 2017 Lire Books

Author Emma Guy Cromwell
Editor Rachel Drice

Originally published 1920.

ISBN-10: 1-939652-81-2
ISBN-13: 978-1-939652-81-2

Book Website: www.LireBooks.com
Email: info@LireBooks.com
Give feedback on the book at: feedback@LireBooks.com

Printed in U.S.A

A Note to Our Readers

To
The New Voters *of* America
A Great Factor in Good Government
This Booklet
is Respectively Dedicated
by
The Author

Historical Perspectives

Taking historical perspective means understanding the social, cultural, intellectual, and emotional settings that shaped people's lives and actions in the past. At any one point, different historical actors may have acted on the basis of conflicting beliefs and ideologies, so understanding diverse perspectives is also a key to historical perspective-taking. Though it is sometimes called "historical empathy," historical perspective is very different from the common-sense notion of identification with another person. Indeed, taking historical perspective demands comprehension of the vast differences between us in the present and those in the past.

Historical Thinking Project
http://historicalthinking.ca/historical-perspectives

CITIZENSHIP

A MANUAL *for* VOTERS

Introduction.

Realizing the need of a manual on citizenship for the new voters in Kentucky, the author has endeavored to compile such information on the government and its workings, as will be of use to all voters, especially the ones just entering political life. A strong appeal is made to the women voters of our nation to prepare themselves for public life by keeping in touch with the issues of the day as well as the functions of government. While it is a great privilege to take part in public affairs, and study the questions of the day, so that we can vote intelligently and criticize justly, let us not forget that the home is the most sacred refuge of life, the nucleus around which all pure and true civilization is formed, and that the chief end of all good government is to improve and protect the home, the church and the community.

Will you take part in building up your government and establishing "High Ideals" and true democracy?

EMMA GUY CROMWELL,
Frankfort, Ky.

one

Citizenship.

Good citizenship means doing well one's part as a member of the community in which he lives, and carries with it certain privileges and duties.

A citizen is one who has the rights and privileges of the inhabitants of the community, state and nation, and as a duty should equip himself so as to render the best citizenship possible.

There are two classes of citizens; native born, and naturalized. Persons born in the United States and children born of American parents while abroad are native born. Naturalized citizens are aliens who through the process of naturalization have attained citizenship. Naturalization itself does not give the right to vote, as that is determined by the state laws. Most states give all citizens the right to vote who have lived in the state for one year, and about eleven states permit aliens to vote provided they declare their intention of becoming citizens.

Congress has the power to decide the conditions upon which aliens may become citizens.

Citizenship carries with it the enjoyment of civil rights, as the protection of the home and property, freedom of speech, religion, press, protection of the laws, etc. Wherever you go your citizenship goes with you, protecting and defending you. If you are in a foreign country you must abide by the laws of that country, but should you be treated unjustly the United States would protect you.

Our country is a land of freedom and opportunity, and it is our duty to help uplift the government, and as citizens we must study conditions and know how to govern and be governed. We must be familiar with our national and state Constitutions, for they are the fundamental principles by which we are governed. We must know how to make laws and how to have them executed. We must keep posted on the issues of the day, and know something of the standing and character of our public men and women.

The citizen who does not possess some knowledge of his government and its workings will become a prey to the demagogue, or of individuals who are anxious to advance their own interest at the expense of the people.

It is the duty of every man and woman under the protection of our flag to give his or her best to the country and be willing to take upon themselves the burden as well as the privilege of government, and fully appreciate the inheritance our fathers left. "They built the foundation in the days of Washington and Jefferson, and as a duty we must safeguard the building."

Citizenship not only embraces civil rights, but political rights which is the right of suffrage or voting.

While civil rights are enjoyed by all men, women and children, political rights are enjoyed only by citizens twenty-one years old and over who possess the necessary qualifications to vote. Civil rights and political rights are not the same, for all citizens are not voters, neither are all voters citizens in the United States, as some states permit aliens to vote before they get their citizenship paper, making them real citizens.

It is our duty to study our government and be posted on the issues of the day. There are about 27,011,330 women voters in the United States. We have the vote and let us not only count it a privilege but a duty to do our part as citizens in establishing good government.

There are two principal parties in the United States, the Democratic party and the Republican party.

The way to get good government is through the parties; that is one reason women must choose their party and enter into the organization of the party of their choice.

Parties are just what their constituents make them.

GOVERNMENT.

The word government means management or guidance and control.

When we speak of the government of the nation, state, city, town or county we refer to the management of public affairs.

Government protects life and property, keeps an army and navy for our defense, peace and order, regulates commerce and industry, supports our public schools, keeps the roads and streets in good condition, cares for public health, and many other things we enjoy.

Our courts are maintained by the government where justice may be found.

The laws of our nation are the rules made by the government to guide our actions. They tell us what we are to do, and what we are not to do. We must obey the laws of our country or else be punished. We must study the government of our nation, state, city, town and county, and be ready to do our part in establishing good government, by making proper laws and seeing they are enforced. As far back as 500 B. C. we find in Athens lawmakers, judges and executive officers.

The word government is derived from the Latin word gubernare, which means to guide or "pilot a ship." Good government depends upon the voters, and may our men and women of the United States pilot our ship into a safe harbor.

The United States is both a Democracy and a Republic.

A Democracy is a government by the people in which the will of the people prevails throughout the country. "This is the fundamental principle of American government."

A Republic is a democracy where the people elect representatives to carry on the government.

CONSTITUTION.

When the colonies became independent states each state drew up a charter which recognized its people as authority in government. Instead of calling this new instrument a charter they changed the name and called it a "Constitution."

This Constitution is the foundation upon which our government is built. After the thirteen original colonies had established their independence they formed a central government known and expressed in the Constitution of the United States which is our fundamental law.

In the preamble of the Constitution of the United States we find the general purpose for which government is instituted:

"We, the people of the United States, in order to form a more perfect union, establish justice, insure domestic tranquility, provide for the common defense, promote the general welfare, and secure the blessings of liberty to ourselves and our posterity, do ordain and establish this Constitution for the United States of America."

The Constitution of the United States is our fundamental law and no state constitution can conflict with our Federal Constitution.

There are now forty-eight states in the United States with forty-eight constitutions framed upon the Federal Constitution. Each state has its own constitution, which in no way conflicts with the Federal Constitution.

The first Constitution of Kentucky was adopted April 3, 1792, at a convention that met in Danville, and later on June 1st, 1792, Kentucky was admitted into the union as a state.

Our government is conducted according to our National and State Constitutions.

In every constitution there is a provision for making a change. These changes are called amendments. An amendment is a law passed by the General Assembly and adopted by a majority of the voters.

An amendment to the Kentucky Constitution requires a three-fifths vote of the members in both houses of the legislature to pass, and then it is submitted by the General Assembly to the voters of the State, which requires a majority of the voters to be adopted.

The legislature cannot repeal an amendment to the Constitution, or pass laws contrary to its provision. The session of nineteen and twenty in Kentucky passed two amendments pertaining to school matters. One provides for the appointment of the Superintendent of Public Instruction by the Governor, and the other amendment provides: "That the General Assembly have the power to distribute the school funds."

At the next general election we will vote on these two amendments. If the majority of the voters vote yes, this change will be made, and the General Assembly will have the power to distribute the school funds and the Governor will appoint the Superintendent of Public Instruction.

The Federal Constitution may be amended by two-thirds vote of each House of Congress, and if passed must be referred to the state legislatures for ratification.

The amendments to the Constitution of the United States do not become a part of the Constitution until ratified by three-fourths of the States, which is now thirty-six states—there being forty-eight states in the union.

There are now eighteen amendments to the Federal Constitution. The nineteenth amendment on "Suffrage" is still pending, needing only one more state to give universal suffrage to women.

An amendment to a constitution is simply changing some of its provisions, but a revision is a recasting of the whole constitution. Both require the consent of the voters of the State.

As we have said the revision usually takes place by means of a convention of delegates elected for that purpose by the people.

"One of the most important parts of every state constitution is the 'Bill of Rights,' which is a statement of the rights which must not be infringed on by the government."

In the revision of a state constitution the legislature submits to the people the question of calling a convention to frame a new constitution. If the voters are in favor of a convention they elect delegates to the convention to assist in revising the constitution. The revised constitution is nearly always submitted to the people to vote upon.

The amendment known as the eighteenth amendment passed during President Wilson's term of office and is one of great importance to our nation in the protection of the home and humanity. This amendment prohibiting the manufacture and sale of intoxicating liquors, reads as follows:

"Sec. 1. After one year from the ratification of this article, the manufacture, sale and transportation of intoxicating liquors within, the importation thereof into, or the exportation thereof from the United States and all territory subject to the jurisdiction thereof for beverage purposes is hereby prohibited.

"Sec. 2. The Congress and the several states shall have concurrent power to enforce this article by appropriate legislation."

There are now eighteen amendments to our Federal Constitution, and there has never been an amendment repealed.

The nineteenth amendment known as the suffrage amendment passed both houses of Congress on May 21st and June 4th, 1919, submitting to the states a proposed amendment to the Federal Constitution extending suffrage to women. The first state to take action was Wisconsin, whose legislature, June 5th, 1919, ratified the amendment. Other state ratifications were Michigan, June 10th, Kansas, New York and Ohio, June 16th, Illinois, June 17th, Pennsylvania, June 24th, Massachusetts, June 25th, Texas, June 28th, Iowa, July 2nd, Missouri, July 3rd, Arkansas, July 28th, Montana, July 30th, Nebraska, August 1st, Minnesota, September 8th, New Hampshire, September 10th, Utah, September 30th, California, November 1st, Maine, November 5th, North Dakota, December 1st, South Dakota, December 4th, Kentucky, January 6th, 1920.

The proposed amendment reads as follows:

"Sec. 1. The right of citizens of the United States to vote shall not be denied or abridged by the United States or by any state on account of sex.

"Sec. 2. Congress shall have power, by appropriate legislation, to enforce the provisions of this article."

The following states had granted state wide woman's suffrage: Wyoming 1869, Colorado 1893, Utah 1896, Idaho 1896, Washington 1910, California 1911, Kansas,

Arizona and Oregon 1912, Territory of Alaska 1913, Montana and Nevada 1914, New York 1917, Michigan, Oklahoma, South Dakota 1918.

Amendments to the Federal Constitution may be proposed by Congress by two-thirds vote, then submitted to the states for ratification by at least three-fourths of the states acting through their legislatures (or through state conventions as Congress may indicate, or Congress may call a national convention for this purpose).

As has been said eighteen amendments to the National Constitution have been made since its adoption. The nineteenth amendment will soon be adopted in full as it only needs one more state to make the three-fourths or thirty-six states which will give us universal suffrage throughout the United States.

Let us remember that the Constitution of the United States is the supreme law of the land, and no law will stand in our courts that is in violation of our National Constitution.

two

Kinds of Government.

For convenience the United States is divided into forty-eight states and each state is divided into counties. Kentucky has one hundred and twenty counties.

We have National, State, county, town and city government.

FEDERAL OR NATIONAL GOVERNMENT.

The Federal or National government, as in state government, is divided into three parts. The legislative which makes the laws. The judicial which interprets or explains the laws. The executive which enforces the laws.

Legislative: The legislative department is called the Congress and is composed of the House of Representatives and the Senate.

The members of the House of Representatives are elected every two years.

The number of representatives in a state is apportioned according to population, and the congressional district from which a member is elected is determined by the legislature of each state.

Kentucky has eleven congressional districts, therefore eleven congressmen elected by the people.

To be a member of the House of Representatives in Congress the man or woman must be twenty-five years old, a citizen of the United States at least seven years, and a resident of the state from which he is chosen. He receives a salary of $7,500 per year, and an allowance for clerk, stationery and traveling expenses.

Every state is entitled to at least one representative. There are now four hundred and thirty-five members in the House of Representatives in Congress.

When the members of a new House of Representatives meet the clerk of the previous House calls them to order and the roll is called by states. If a quorum is present they elect a speaker from among the members of the House who takes his seat immediately. The other officers are elected as the clerk, sergeant-at-arms and doorkeeper. The rules of the House define the duties of the speaker.

The work of the House of Representatives is done through committees. When a bill is introduced it is referred to a committee and this committee may report it back to the House either favorably or unfavorably, or they may not report it at all. If reported favorably it has a chance of receiving consideration.

Much of the work of Congress is done in the committee rooms. This is why the selection of committees is so important.

When a bill is reported favorably by a committee it is placed upon the calendar which is a register of bills. Then the fate of the bill rests with the rules committee of the House.

The committee on rules, as other committees, is elected by the House. The party in power usually determines the selection of this committee.

Impeachment: If a high official is charged with misconduct in office the House of Representatives would impeach him and if found guilty, the impeachment is carried to the Senate to be tried. The U. S. Senate sits as a court of justice.

Six judges, one President and one Secretary of War have been impeached by the House of Representatives.

Revenue: All bills for raising revenue must originate in the House of Representatives.

United States Senate.

The Senate has ninety-six members, two from every state in the union, and are elected for six years, receiving a salary of $7,500 a year. The presiding officer of the Senate is the Vice President of the United States.

The United States Senators are elected by the direct voice of the voters of the state according to the 17th amendment to the National Constitution passed in 1913.

A United States Senator must be thirty years old, a citizen of the United States for nine years, and must live in the state from which he is elected.

The term of office of only one-third of the Senators expires at the same time, so at least two-thirds of the Senate is not new.

The Senate must confirm all appointments made by the President and must ratify all treaties made by him with a two-thirds vote.

Bills originate in the Senate in the same way as in the House, referred to a committee and their course is directly the same. When passed by both Houses the President has ten days to sign or veto them. Without his signature they become a law, unless Congress by adjourning prevents the return within ten days.

The committees of the Senate are elected by its members.

Bills are passed in Congress similar to that in the legislature of a state. They are introduced by a member in either house and must pass both houses, then signed by the presiding officers and clerks and go to the President for his signature or veto.

The sessions are yearly, beginning on the first Monday in December, and last until March 4th; this is known as the short session. The long session occurs in odd numbered years and continues until it is adjourned. The President has the power to call special sessions of Congress.

Judicial Department.

The Federal courts derive their powers and jurisdiction from the Constitution and laws of the United States.

"The judicial powers of the United States shall be vested in one Supreme Court, and in such inferior courts as Congress may from time to time establish."

The Supreme Court of the United States is the highest and most powerful judicial body in the world.

It holds its regular sessions at Washington, sitting from October to July.

The chief justice and eight associate justices constitute the Supreme Court of the United States, and are appointed for life by the President of the United States and confirmed by the United States Senate.

The salary of the chief justice is $15,000.00 per year, and of the associate justices $14,000.00 per year.

Six judges must be present in the trial of a case and a majority is necessary in rendering a decision.

The district judges receive a salary of $6,000.00 annually and the judges of the appeals court $7,000.00 annually.

The judges cannot be removed except for cause, and then they are impeached in the House of Representatives and tried in the United States Senate.

The principal Federal courts that have been organized by Congress are: The Supreme Court, the Circuit Court of Appeals, the Circuit Court, the District Court.

A United States judge if he has served ten years may retire on full salary when seventy years old.

EXECUTIVE DEPARTMENT.

The most important offices in the United States are the President and Vice President. They are legally elected by electors chosen by the voters of the forty-eight states.

The President of the United States must be a natural born citizen living in this country for fourteen years at least, and must be thirty-five years old.

He is elected for four years and receives a salary of $75,000.00 annually and residence. Congress makes other allowances for expenses.

The President is the Commander in Chief of the army and navy. He appoints every administrative officer except the Vice President. He may call extra sessions, and may veto bills, which Congress can pass over his veto with a two-thirds majority in each House. He represents the United States in all dealings with foreign powers.

The President appoints the members of his cabinet, but said appointments must be approved by the United States Senate.

The Cabinet consist of a Secretary of State, Treasury, War, Navy, Agriculture, Commerce, Labor, Interior, the Attorney General and Postmaster General.

Each member of the Cabinet receives a salary of $12,000.00 annually.

The Secretary of State is the first in rank among the Cabinet officers, and in case of the death of the President and Vice President would succeed to the office of President.

The financial manager of the national government is the Secretary of the Treasury.

The Secretary of War has charge of the military affairs of the nation under the direction of the President. He also looks after river and harbor improvements, and all obstructions to navigation.

The Attorney General is the chief law officer of the government.

The Postmaster General has charge of the Post Office Department.

The Secretary of Navy has charge of the construction and equipment of vessels of war.

The Secretary of Interior has charge of matters pertaining to the internal welfare of the nation, as public lands, care of national parks, the giving of patents for inventions, Indian affairs, education, etc.

The Secretary of Agriculture promotes the general agricultural interests of the country.

The Secretary of Commerce promotes the commercial interest of the nation.

The Secretary of Labor promotes and develops the welfare of the wage earner of the United States, by improving the working conditions and advancing their opportunities for better employment.

The Vice President of the United States must have the same qualifications as the President.

He receives a salary of $12,000.00 annually.

TREATIES.

The framers of the National Constitution gave the United States Senate two important executive powers especially—first, approving treaties. Second, confirming appointments made by the President. All treaties in order to be ratified must receive a two-thirds vote of the Senators present when the vote was taken.

When a treaty has been drawn up the President consults with the Committee on Foreign Relations and the Senate. "Treaties are considered in secret session. The Senate may approve or reject a treaty as a whole; or they may ratify it in part by recommending additional articles as amendments, but the treaty does not become a law until the President and the foreign power agree to the amendment."

While the Senate may approve, reject or change the terms of a treaty, all changes must be agreed to by the President and the nation interested. When accepted by both nations duplicate parchment copies are made, and both copies are signed by the chief officers of each country and then exchanged. This is called the "exchange of ratification." Each nation secures an official copy of the treaty. The President publishes the treaty followed by a proclamation.

The Constitution gives the President the power to negotiate treaties and conventions with foreign countries. He conducts the negotiation through the department of Secretary of State. The President keeps in touch and consults with the Committee on Foreign Relations and with the majority of the leaders in the Senate during negotiations.

"The President shall have power, by and with the advice and consent of the Senate, to make treaties, provided two-thirds of the Senators present concur."

The Federal Constitution makes treaties a part of the supreme law of the land. Any conflicting provision of a state law or Constitution is repealed.

The League of Nations having failed to get the necessary two-thirds vote in the United States Senate so far has not become a law. It is opposed by a few senators which prevented it receiving the two-thirds vote.

CIVIL SERVICE.

A great number of our offices of government are appointed and not elected. Over 300,000 positions are filled under the national government appointment. On

January 16th, 1883, Congress passed the Civil Service law which established a United States Civil Service Commission composed of three members, of which not more than two should belong to the same political party. The commission is appointed by the President with the consent of the Senate.

The ordinary "Civil Service" examinations are held twice a year at different places in the country designated by the commission.

This commission appoints boards of examiners who hold examinations at least twice a year at Washington, D. C., and in the states and territories.

The commission encourages efficiency by promotion from lower to higher grades of public service. Some of the places that come under the civil service system are clerks in Washington connected with the national government, officials in the postal service, the letter carriers and clerks in post offices and railway mail service, employees in custom houses, government printing office, Indian service and revenue service.

Senators and representatives are not allowed to recommend any applicant to the board of examiners appointed by the commission.

The examinations are practical and the questions pertain to the nature of the work the applicant is to do.

Persons employed in such public service are under obligations not to contribute to any political fund, or to render service to any political party.

three

State Government.

The state constitution adopted by the voters is the fundamental law of the state.

A state Constitution cannot interfere with the Federal Constitution, neither can the Federal Constitution interfere with the regulation of the state. As has been said the Kentucky Constitution was adopted on April 3, 1792, at a convention which met in Danville.

A state Constitution is a law made by the people and cannot be changed by the legislature, but may be amended or revised by the voters.

Amendments are usually submitted to the legislature and then to the voters.

The revision of the Constitution is by means of a convention of delegates elected by the people.

The three departments of state governments are: The legislative, the lawmaking power; the judicial, the law interpreting power; and the executive, the law enforcing power.

All state governments are divided into these three classes, the legislative, judicial and executive.

The legislature passes laws which govern people in their relation to each other.

The Kentucky legislature convenes at the capital at Frankfort every two years on the first Tuesday after the first Monday in January and remains in session for sixty working days, not including Sundays and national holidays.

It is composed of two houses, the House of Representatives, known as the lower house with one hundred members, and the Senate, known as the upper house with thirty-eight members.

The Kentucky General Assembly is composed of one hundred and thirty-eight members elected by the voters of the State in the counties and districts in which they reside.

The State is divided into senatorial and representative districts, with a representation based upon population.

The term of office for Senators is four years. A Senator must be thirty years old, a citizen of the United States for nine years and must live in the State and district from which he is elected.

A State Senator in Kentucky receives $10.00 per day for his services during the sitting of the legislature, mileage to and from home at the rate of ten cents per mile, and stationery.

The Lieutenant Governor is the presiding officer of the Senate.

The Senate sits as a court and tries all impeachments.

The president pro tem. of the Senate is elected by the members of the body, also the clerks, doorkeeper and pages.

The president pro tem. presides in the absence of the Lieutenant Governor, and in case of vacancy to this office would become Lieutenant Governor.

The president of the Senate appoints the standing committees, unless the opposite party is in power, then the president pro tem. virtually controls said appointments.

To be a member of the House of Representatives a person must be twenty-four years old.

His term of office is only two years but he receives the same salary as a Senator, $10.00 per day, mileage and stationery.

The body elects its speaker and other officers, and has the sole power of impeachment.

The principal work in both houses are done through the committees appointed by the President of the Senate and Speaker of the House.

A bill is prepared and introduced by a member of the Senate or House. If it pertains to revenue and taxation, it must originate in the House of Representatives.

When a bill is introduced the clerk of the body reads it by title only. The President of the Senate or Speaker of the House then refers it to the proper committee (of the body in which the bill originated). It is numbered and ordered printed when referred to the committee. The committee considers the bill and usually reports it back with expression of opinion that it should or should not pass to the body in which it originated. (The committee may pigeonhole it and not report it, or may report it too late for action by the body.)

The bill and the report from the committee is printed and placed on the calendar and takes its turn to be brought up for passage. (By consent a bill is acted upon out of its turn.)

The bill is taken in its regular order from the calendar and read the second time in full by the clerk. It is open to debate or amendment unless the previous question is ordered, which if adopted cuts off debate and amendment. Then the bill is read the third time by title only. (Any member may demand the reading in full of the engrossed bill if he desires.) It is then placed on its passage by the presiding officer of the body, and if passed it is then transmitted to the Senate by the House clerk, if a House bill. If a Senate bill, it is taken by the Senate clerk to the House for consideration.

A bill goes through the same form in either body, after which it is returned to the body in which it originated with or without amendments. If the bill is passed it goes into possession of the clerk of the body in which it originated. Then the enrolling clerk of the body in which the bill originated enrolls it verbatim from the original. After it is enrolled it is compared by the committee on enrollment in each House. If found correctly enrolled the chairman of each committee reports it to the body, and it is compared again by the clerks of each body and signed by the clerk of the body in which it originated, also signed by the President of the Senate and the Speaker of the House. (The presiding officer of the House in which it originated signs first.) Then the clerk of that body takes it to the Governor for his approval. If the Governor approves it he does so with his signature. It becomes a law at once if it has an emergency clause; otherwise, in ninety days after its signature by the Governor. It is then filed with the Secretary of State. Then later on the bills passed during the session are compiled by the Attorney General and known as the Acts of the General Assembly of that session. If the Governor vetoes a bill while the Legislature is in session, it may be taken up in the house in which it originated, and passed over his veto, but must receive a two-thirds vote in each house.

The Governor is allowed ten days after the General Assembly adjourns for approving bills, and if not signed within that time they become the law without his signature.

The passage of a bill in all the states is about the same.

four

Judiciary Department.

The state courts derive their powers and jurisdiction from the Constitution and laws of the state. The courts in different states go by different names, yet the jurisdiction is about the same.

The Court of Appeals is the highest court in Kentucky. It holds annual sessions from about September fifteenth to about June twenty-second at the State Capitol, Frankfort, Kentucky.

Seven judges and one commissioner constitute the Court of Appeals in Kentucky, and each receives a salary of five thousand dollars per year, a clerk or secretary and an office furnished in the new capitol building.

A person to be a member of the Court of Appeals must be thirty-five years old and a citizen of the State for five years. He must have resided two years in the judicial district from which he is elected.

The Court of Appeals or Supreme Court is the highest court of the State. This court is the State court of last resort.

The judges of the Court of Appeals are elected by the people for a term of eight years, commencing on the first Monday in January succeeding their election.

The cases tried before the Court of Appeals are usually appealed to it from the lower courts.

There are certain classes of cases that come before the Court of Appeals for first trial in which is involved the question of official action of State officers.

CIRCUIT COURT.

The circuit judge holds this court first in one county and then in another until the circuit of the counties which compose his district is completed.

Circuit court is held in the court house of the county seat two or three times a year, presided over by the judge of that district elected by the voters. (In case of a vacancy the Governor of the State appoints some lawyer to fill his place.) The majority of important cases are tried in this court, because a jury trial may always be had in the circuit court.

The Constitution of the United States provides that every man or woman shall have the right to trial by jury in all criminal cases, and in civil cases involving a sum of more than $20.00.

Twelve citizens known as a grand jury usually meet at the time the circuit court convenes. All violations of law are investigated, and persons found guilty are indicted by the grand jury.

COUNTY COURT.

The county court is held at the county seat of every county and is presided over by the county judge. The county judge is elected by the voters of the county.

In this court civil suits are tried in which the sum involved is not over $200.00. It tries the more important cases which do not come before the justice of the peace court, or city police court.

The county judge's office is the most important office in the county. He probates wills and appoints executors, administrators, and guardians. He is the head of the fiscal court which looks after all the material interests of the county, as construction of roads, care of paupers and the general interest of the county.

JUSTICE OF THE PEACE COURT.

The justice of the peace court is the lowest court and is held by a justice of peace, called a magistrate, who is elected in that magisterial district by the voters. Petty misdemeanors involving small sums of money are tried in this court.

The justices' courts are found in every community for protection and convenience to the people.

The magistrates are members of the fiscal court of the county.

POLICE COURT.

The police courts in towns and cities are similar to the justices' courts. They are necessary in every city to try the petty misdemeanors. A police judge is elected by the voters of the city and tries all petty cases under his jurisdiction.

JURIES.

The grand jury is selected by the court and is composed of not less than twelve responsible and qualified citizens. It is their duty to make a faithful inquiry into all wrongs and violations of the law. They call witnesses before them and make an investigation, and upon sufficient proof against a person they have them indicted. The proceedings of a grand jury are secret.

The terms "jury" and trial by jury are quite different from a grand jury. The grand jury investigates and inquires into all wrongs and violations of the law and if the person accused is guilty returns an indictment. Then the trial jury of twelve persons after hearing the evidence given them in court returns their unanimous verdict one way or other, otherwise a hung jury.

There is a difference between a trial by jury and a grand jury. The petit jury or trial by jury is composed of twelve men, honest and upright citizens living within the jurisdictional limits of the court, drawn and selected by officers free from all biased opinion and sworn to render a true verdict according to the law and evidence given them. Every citizen is entitled to a fair trial, even though the accused is known to be guilty. The Constitution of the United States gives this right to all citizens.

The trial of all crimes shall be by jury except in impeachment. The Constitution provides that the trial be held in the state where the crime is committed, and if the crime is not committed in any of the states Congress has the power to name a place of trial.

The jurors decide whether or not the party accused is guilty by a unanimous vote, and if one or more vote against, it is called a hung jury.

The judge of the court instructs the jurors on the law in the case.

EXECUTIVE DEPARTMENT.

The executive department of state government is the law enforcing power.

The governor of a state is the chief executive. His duty is to see that the laws of his state are executed, to study the conditions and needs of the state, and to prepare a message to the legislature setting forth these needs and conditions. He is commander in chief of the state militia.

He should fill all vacancies that come under his appointing power, appoint certain state officers and boards, grant pardon to convicted criminals when right, call a special session of the legislature when necessary.

The governor represents his state in its relation to the federal government and to other states.

The Governor of Kentucky receives a salary of six thousand and five hundred dollars per year, all expenses when on duty for the State, and in addition, a mansion lighted, heated, and furnished, and three thousand dollars per year for public entertaining. He is elected for four years and cannot succeed himself for re-election.

Most of the states have the following state officials elected by the voters of the state: Governor, Lieutenant Governor, Secretary of State, Treasurer, Auditor, Attorney General, Commissioner of Agriculture and Superintendent of Public Instruction.

The Superintendent of Public Instruction, the Attorney General and the Secretary of State compose the Board of Education.

COUNTY GOVERNMENT.

The county is a political division created by the state to administer local affairs, to act as agent for the state, to collect taxes, and enforce state laws.

The county owns many of the public buildings such as the court house and jail.

Every state is divided into counties, and every village, town or city is located in some county. As has been said there are one hundred and twenty counties in the State of Kentucky. The county seat of a county is where the business of a county is transacted, and where the courts of importance are held. It is really the capital of the county.

Some counties on account of size and population have two county seats. While county government differs in many states there is a uniformity in the organization of counties throughout the union.

A county judge is elected in every county by the people. He presides over the county court which is held at the county seat.

Some of the other officers of the county elected by the voters are: The sheriff, county superintendent of schools, circuit clerk, clerk of the county court, coroner, prosecuting attorney, county attorney, tax commissioner.

Town Government.

The government of a town is perhaps the nearest approach we have to a direct government by the people themselves.

Towns as well as counties not only look after their local interest but look after state interest within their boundaries.

A community of three hundred or more may upon petition of two-thirds of its inhabitants, be incorporated as a town.

Towns as well as counties are organized and governed under general laws passed by the legislature of its state.

The incorporated township has a right to hold property and make contracts.

CITY GOVERNMENT.

Cities like towns and counties receive their right of government through the state by a charter granted by the state legislature. The charter is the fundamental law of the city.

The chief executive officer of a city is the mayor who is generally elected by the people.

The power of city government is vested in the mayor and the city council.

For convenience a city is divided into subdivisions called wards, and for elections into certain voting precincts called election districts.

The board of aldermen or council is composed of one person chosen from each ward by the voters. Their power is limited by the city charter.

Voters are responsible for their government and much of our happiness depends upon the way our city is managed.

Many cities have adopted the commission form of government by electing a non-partisan ticket composed of several commissioners. Each commissioner is put in charge of a division of the city's administration and held responsible for the work of his department.

The mayor of a city presides over the meetings of the council and sometimes vetos measures passed. He is elected by the voters. The chief duty of the mayor is to see that the laws and ordinances are enforced.

In large cities there is a system of courts extending from the police court to the higher courts.

Appeals from the courts of the city are taken to the circuit court and may go from there to the Supreme Court of the State.

Cities are divided into six classes in Kentucky:

First class having a population of 100,000 or over.

Second class, 20,000 to 100,000.

Third class, 8,000 to 20,000.

Fourth class, 3,000 to 8,000.

Fifth class, 1,000 to 3,000.

Sixth class, below 1,000.

five

Party Organization.

The difference of opinion on national questions is the cause of a number of political parties in the United States.

As long as men and women think for themselves we shall have political parties.

It is really the product of a government by public opinion. Without political organizations it would be almost impossible to govern the policy and character of the country and control the affairs of the nation.

The political parties are the agents through which organizations are made.

As a test of one's love of his country and its government is shown by his work and aggressiveness.

Every citizen should study the ethics of his government, think for himself, and form his own opinion.

A person with no opinion on public affairs is a coward and unpatriotic.

Our nation depends largely upon moral and cultured people who will study the issues of the day and express themselves in positive terms on what they deem best for the nation and its government.

Organization is a number of people systematically united for some end. It is through organization that political parties become effective.

Political parties arose after the adoption of the Constitution. They are organized for national, state and local campaigns, and not originally a part of the government, but as we grew and the population became greater there arose different political parties. Every district, village, town and city has its permanent local campaign committees in elections, beside the state and national committees, which make a very complete organization.

The duty of the permanent committees is to keep the machinery of the party working. Really the permanent committees do the hard work in politics. They organize political clubs, solicit funds, issue calls for conventions, urge people to register and vote and in many other ways keep up the interest of the party.

Since the adoption of the Constitution there have been two principal parties advocating different principles.

The first parties were known as the Federalist and anti-Federalist.

The two great dominant parties now in the United States—the Democratic and Republican parties.

Our Constitution did not provide us with laws as to the way of selecting candidates for office, but just as soon as political parties came into existence, nominations followed.

DEMOCRATIC PARTY.

The Democratic party is the oldest. It goes back to the days of Jefferson. It advocated "state rights," limiting the power of national government, tariff for revenue only. These were some of the issues discussed before the recent war, but other important issues in these days of reconstruction have taken their place.

REPUBLICAN PARTY.

The Republican party was formed before the Civil War, when Abraham Lincoln was elected President of the United States. It was originally called the Federalist party.

The Republican party remained in control of the national government until 1884 Grover Cleveland was elected for two terms, four years each.

This party originally advocated a high tariff.

The recent platforms of the two parties now in power will give the issues of the present day.

six

Committees.

The national committee of each party is formed of one member from each state, who organizes the national convention of his party.

The chairman of this committee of each party calls a meeting of his committee in the spring before the presidential election and decides when and where they will hold the national convention.

This year the Democratic convention was held in San Francisco, beginning on 28th of June.

The Republican convention was held in Chicago on the 8th of June.

Each convention adopted its own party platform.

DEMOCRATIC.

STATE CENTRAL COMMITTEE OF KENTUCKY.

The State Central Committee is the party organization in control of the party in the State. It is composed of one man from each of the eleven congressional districts elected by the people and a member at large.

MEMBERS OF STATE CENTRAL COMMITTEE FROM KENTUCKY.

State at Large—George B. Martin, Catlettsburg.

State Executive Committee from State at Large—J. A. Robinson, Lancaster.

STATE CENTRAL COMMITTEE BY DISTRICTS.

1st District—Arch Nelson............................Marshall Co. (Benton)

2nd District—Ira D. Smith................Christian Co. (Hopkinsville)

3rd District—T. P. Dickerson........................Barren Co. (Glasgow)

4th District—W. C. Montgomery.....Hardin Co. (Elizabethtown)

5th District—Henry J. Tilford................Jefferson Co. (Louisville)

6th District—Judge Otto Wolfe.............Campbell Co. (Newport)

7th District—Thos P. Middleton................Henry Co. (Eminence)

8th District—J. H. Nichols.............................Boyle Co. (Danville)

9th District—Foster B. Cox.............Jessamine Co. (Nicholasville)

10th District—J. R. Johnson.............................Pike Co. (Pikeville)

11th District—Edward Gatcliff.........Whitley Co. (Williamsburg)

DEMOCRATIC STATE EXECUTIVE COMMITTEE.

1st District—Thomas Turner...Trigg Co. (Cadiz)

2nd District—John L. Dorsey...Henderson Co. (Henderson)

3rd District—Dr. Joe M. Ferguson........Muhlenberg (Greenville)

4th District—Chas. Hubbard..................Larue Co. (Hodgenville)

5th District—Fred Forcht......................Jefferson Co. (Louisville)

6th District—W. N. Hind........................Kenton Co. (Covington)

7th District—W. T. Klair...........................Fayette Co. (Lexington)

8th District—Dr. T. R. Welch........Jessamine Co. (Nicholasville)

9th District—Dr. J. D. Whitaker..........Morgan Co. (Whitesburg)

10th District—Bailey P. Wooten......................Perry Co. (Hazard)

11th District—Cecil Williams..................Pulaski Co. (Somerset)

Chairman Democratic National Committee, Homer S. Cummings, Baltimore, Md.

REPUBLICAN.
STATE CENTRAL COMMITTEE OF KENTUCKY.

Chas. H. Searcy, Chairman...Louisville, Ky.

R. W. Hunter, Vice Chairman...................................Providence, Ky.

Lilburn Phelps, Secretary..Louisville, Ky.

Mrs. Lillian Davis, Assistant Secretary......................Louisville, Ky.

Elliott Callahan, Treasurer...Louisville, Ky.

NATIONAL COMMITTEEMEN.

A. T. Hert..Louisville, Ky.

At Large—Maurice L. Galvin....................................Covington, Ky.

At Large—R. W. Hunter..Providence, Ky.

At Large—Mrs. John W. Langley..................................Pikeville, Ky.

At Large—Ed. W. Chenault.......................................Lexington, Ky.

1st District—W. L. Prince...Benton, Ky.

2nd District—Virgil Y. Moore...............................Madisonville, Ky.

3rd District—Clayton C. Curd..................................Greenville, Ky.

4th District—D. O. Burke.. Bradfordville, Ky.

5th District—J. Matt Chilton...................................... Louisville, Ky.

6th District—G. A. Seiler...Covington, Ky.

7th District—Clarence Miller...Irvine, Ky.

8th District—H. V. Bastin...Lancaster, Ky.

9th District—F. A. Field..Ashland, Ky.

10th District—Sam Collins.....................................Whitesburg, Ky.

11th District—Chas. Finley....................................Williamsburg, Ky.

County Committee.

The county committee consists of one man or woman from each elective district in the county, and the city committee one from each ward or election district in the city.

County Convention.

The voters of the county of the party they represent meet at the court house at the county seat and elect a temporary chairman and the delegates to represent the party at the State convention.

If the people of the county favor a certain man for President they may instruct their delegates for this man in the State convention.

The fight at the convention is usually for chairman, who when elected usually appoints a committee to draw resolutions and names the delegates in the resolutions, which are reported back to the convention for action.

State Convention.

The call for State convention is issued by the State Central Committee of the party, and a copy of the call is sent to the chairman of each local committee. The convention is called to order by the chairman of the State Committee.

The secretary of the State Central Committee reads the call of the convention.

The convention is opened with prayer.

Motions are made that the chair appoint a committee on credentials, on permanent organization, and on resolutions.

A temporary chairman and secretary are elected.

The report of the committee on credentials is read, giving the number of delegates present, and rendering a decision concerning contested delegations.

The report of the committee on organization is usually adopted at once and names the permanent officers of the convention, which include a permanent chairman, secretary, assistant secretaries, vice chairman and sergeant-at-arms.

The chairman of the convention is generally a prominent party leader, and when he takes his seat he delivers a speech upon the issues of the campaign.

The platform is read by the chairman of the committee on resolutions and usually accepted without amendments. Then the convention takes up the nomination of candidates. After the nominations are made the vote is then taken by call of the counties by the secretary. When the candidates receive the number necessary to elect, generally a majority of all the votes cast, some one usually moves that his nomination be made unanimous. They elect all the officers in the same way.

seven

National Convention.

The National Convention is called to order about noon on the day appointed in the official call, by the chairman of the national committee.

The convention is opened with prayer.

The call is read, after which the national committee names a list of temporary officers for the convention, temporary chairman, secretary, clerks, sergeant-at-arms and stenographers.

The temporary chairman takes the chair and makes a formal speech on the political situation.

A resolution is adopted making the rules of the preceding convention the rules of the convention until otherwise ordered.

Motions are made for the appointment of committees on credentials, permanent organization, rules and resolutions, each consisting of one member from each state and territory.

Resolutions concerning contested seats are presented to the convention and referred without debate to the committee on credentials. (Every state is allowed double as many delegates as it has Senators and Representatives in Congress. The four men corresponding to the representation of the Senate are delegates at large, the others are district delegates, which number twenty-two district delegates and four delegates at large, making twenty-six delegates to the National Convention from Kentucky.)

This ends the first session of the convention.

When the convention assembles for the second session, the first business is the report of the credential committee.

In deciding contested seats, the committee on credentials gives each side a chance to present its claims, and then decides between them, generally in favor of the regular delegates, those endorsed by the state and the district committee.

Two full contesting delegations from the same state, sometimes seats are given to both, each delegate being entitled to one-half vote.

After the credential committee arrives at a decision concerning contested seats, its report including a list arranged by the states of all delegates entitled to seats is usually accepted by the convention with very little debate.

Then the committee on organization make their report, which consists of a list of permanent officers of the convention—previously arranged to some extent by the national committee. (This report is usually arranged beforehand and therefore adopted without much trouble, if any.) A committee is appointed to escort the permanent chairman to the platform, who usually delivers a speech on the issues of the coming campaign.

The chair calls for the committee on rules first, for their report.

Two rules of great importance in a Democratic Convention are: First—A rule requiring for the nomination of candidates two-thirds of the whole number of votes in the convention. The Republican requires only a majority.

Second Rule—The so-called unit rule under which a majority of each state delegation is allowed to cast the entire vote to which the state is entitled even against the protest of a minority of the delegation. These two rules are strictly adhered to in the Democratic party only.

While waiting on the resolution committee's report, miscellaneous business is disposed of, such as the election of national committees and of committees on notification. Such committees usually consist of one delegate from each state and territory, the members being designated by the respective delegations.

About the third day the resolution committee is ready to report the platform.

This platform is a formal statement of the party's attitude upon the public questions of the day; next to the nomination of candidates it is the most important work of the convention.

The platform of any party is usually adopted as read.

Nominations for candidates are next in order, and these begin with the roll call of the states arranged alphabetically for the presentation of candidates for the presidential nomination. Several candidates are often nominated. The delegation from any state when called in its turn may pass its right of nomination to any other delegation not yet called.

Some good and influential speaker will nominate the candidate from his state, and it is usually seconded by a good speaker from some state that has not a candidate.

After roll call for nominations is completed the convention proceeds to the first ballot.

The chairman of the delegation from his state when the state is called by the secretary of the convention, arises and announces the vote of his state. Sometimes a candidate is nominated by acclamation, but usually many ballots are necessary to decide the contest.

If a candidate is not nominated on the first few ballots, a dark horse sometimes receives the nomination, but this is seldom the case.

As soon as a candidate receives the number of votes necessary to nominate, which is two-thirds of the delegates in a Democratic convention and a majority in a Republican convention, usually some one moves that the nomination be made unanimous, which is adopted with great applause.

After the nomination for President is over the convention proceeds in the same way to nominate a candidate for Vice President.

At the national convention of each party a new national committee is appointed to carry on the campaign and act until the next convention.

The platform adopted at the national convention of either party is an expression of the principles of the party.

Sometimes a plank is put in to catch voters. On some questions the plank may not be plain, but may straddle the issues.

The national platform gives the principles to which the party is committed and its attitude on important public questions.

eight

Registration.

In all cities where registration of the voters is required, men and women register on the same day in the ward or precinct in which they live.

For the purpose of registration the polls open from 6 o'clock a. m. to 9 o'clock p. m.

There are four election officers who have a book in which are registered the names of all the legal voters in their precinct. Two of these officers are called judges; one is a sheriff and the other is a clerk.

A person desiring to register enters the voting place and announces his or her intention to register. The judge takes the name, residence, party affiliation and citizenship, and may also inquire as to any other matter that would affect his or her right to vote at an election.

If found to be qualified, that is 21 years of age and a resident of the state for one year, a resident of the county for six months, and a resident of the precinct for sixty days, they may register unless in a class prohibited by law from exercising the right to vote.

The clerk then writes the name and address in the registration book entering also color and political affiliation. When this is done the registration is completed, and the elector is qualified to exercise the right of suffrage in all subsequent elections, special elections and primary elections for one year. The officers of the election give him or her a certificate of registration signed by all four officers of the registration, and if they lose this certificate they cannot vote at the regular election unless they get a duplicate certificate from the county clerk, which costs 50 cents.

In the different class cities there are some differences as to the method and time of registering, but in Kentucky the general registration is usually on the first Tuesday of October, in all cities and towns of the first, second, third, fourth and fifth classes. The hours for registration are from six o'clock a. m. to nine o'clock p. m.

Special registrations are held thereafter as follows: One special registration may be held by order of the city authorities, which will be conducted exactly as the first registration above referred to, and during the Monday, Tuesday and Wednesday next preceding the general election day those persons who were absent or sick, or unable to attend and register on the regular registration days, may appear before the county court clerk at his office in the court house, and register, to have the same effect as if the registration had taken place in the manner above referred to, also on the day before the election and on election day, public officers of the state, and the United States government, traveling salesmen and certain ministers of religion may apply before the county court clerk in the court house and be registered if they will make oath that they were not present in their city or town during any of the previous registration days. Persons that have become eligible to vote at the general primary election, which occurs on the first Saturday in August may register two weeks before the election in the county court clerk's office as above described, provided such persons were not in the city on any of the previous regular registration days, or who were not then qualified to register and may vote in the primary election in the same manner as other qualified electors.

The primary election is conducted in the same manner as any other election.

When you register the clerk gives you a certificate of registration, which you keep to show the election officers when you go to vote, that you have registered.

Persons living in the country and small towns do not have to register.

The names of all candidates are arranged in columns, under the party device to which they belong. A voter by putting a cross mark in the circle under the rooster votes for all the Democratic nominees of his party. In

Name of voter........................ Consecutive number..........

Residence..

UNITED STATES

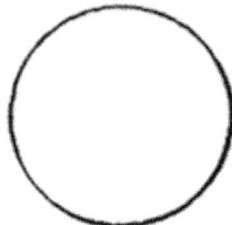

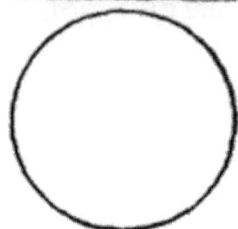

DEMOCRATIC PARTY   **REPUBLICAN PARTY**

For Presidential Electors   For Presidential Electors

.....................................☐   ....☐

.....................................☐   ....☐

For Vice-Presidential Electors   For Vice-Presidential Electors

.....................................☐   ....☐

.....................................☐   ....☐

the circle under the log cabin votes for the Republican nominees of his party.

This does not require a knowledge to even read, only to be able to distinguish between the pictures of a rooster and a log cabin.

NOMINATIONS—PRIMARIES.

Candidates in the United States are usually nominated either in a party primary or a nominating convention.

Primaries are conducted like elections. The name of the party running for an office is put on the ballot of his party with the names of others who have filed similar petitions. On the day set for the primary the voters go to the polls and cast their vote as at a general election. The candidate who receives the largest number of votes is the nominee of the party for that office.

Primaries cost more than conventions—they are like elections—you have to advertise extensively and meet the voters. In a few months the election follows and you practically go over the same.

Only the voters who can vote in the party primary are those who registered for the previous election as members of that party.

Certificates and petitions of nomination must be filed with the Secretary of State not more than seventy-five days and not less than forty-five days, before the day fixed by law for the election of the persons in nomination, also certificates and petitions are directed to be filed with the clerk of the county court not more than seventy-five and not less than forty-five days before the election.

The primary elections are conducted in the same manner as any other election.

The two methods of making nominations are by a caucus or convention system, and the primary election system.

The qualifications for a voter at a primary are the same as election. On the first Saturday in August each year from 6 o'clock a. m. to 4 o'clock p. m. there shall be held at the regular polling places in each election precinct a primary election for the nomination of candidates for office by political parties, to be voted for at the next November election. You do not register to vote in the primary, and a citizen not of age at the time of the primary, but will be twenty-one before the November election can vote in the primary.

Primaries are conducted similar to elections—about same laws and regulations.

ELECTIONS.

After all the political parties have nominated their candidates then the struggle for election begins.

The period of a few months between the nominations and elections is spent by each party in trying to get votes for its candidate.

Every voter must be twenty-one years old, a resident of the state for one year, of the county six months, and of the precinct sixty days.

On election day the voter goes to the polling place and appears before the election officers, who will probably be the same ones who presided at the registration. You give your name and residence, and if you live in a city where registration is required you must produce your registration certificate and one of the judges may consult the registration book to see if you have registered. If found to be registered, the clerk will write your name and address upon the stub of the ballot book and endorse his own name on the back of the ballot, and remove the ballot from the book leaving the stub (called the primary stub) in the book.

The voter will go into a voting booth with the ballot folded, then unfold the ballot, take the stencil, press it on the ink pad and if you desire to vote a straight party ticket place the stencil mark in the circle immediately underneath the device of the party whose candidates you desire to vote for. If you desire to vote for candidates irrespective of any party affiliation you will place the stencil mark in the small square immediately following the name of each candidate for whom you desire to vote.

When the ballot is thus completed you lay the stencil aside, fold the ballot in exactly the same manner as when you received it from the clerk and then return it to the judge of the election, who removes the secondary stub from the ballot and deposits the ballot itself in the ballot box. If any voter spoils or defaces a ballot by mistake so that it cannot be used he may return it, and get another, and the fact noted by the clerk by writing the word "spoiled" on the stub and spoiled ballot.

No person except the election officers shall remain within fifty feet of the polls, except when voting.

It shall be the duty of the sheriff in each county before an election to secure in each precinct of the county a suitable room in which to hold the election, and have sufficient booths in which electors shall mark their ballots, screened from observation.

Our laws concerning elections are more stringent in the past few years. Every precaution is taken to insure honesty of elections.

No officer of election shall do any electioneering on election day.

In all elections in Kentucky the voting shall be by ballot.

The ballot boxes are opened and inspected before voting begins to see that they are empty.

Electioneering is forbidden within one hundred feet of the polls.

Twice as many official ballots are provided for every polling place as there are registered voters in the district.

If a person is illiterate he is allowed assistance in marking his ballot.

An inspector may challenge a person's vote, but if they swear they are eligible their vote is recorded and marked challenged.

A person cannot vote who is not naturalized for at least ninety days before election. Also a person convicted of bribery or an infamous crime, a deserter from the army or navy, and one who bets on that election cannot vote.

The Governor of the State may restore one to citizenship so that they can vote.

In registration polls are opened from 6 a. m. to 9 p. m., but in election polls are opened from 6 a. m. to 4 p. m.

When the polls are closed the ballots are counted by the election officers and announced and placed in ballot box, which is locked by officers, who then take the ballot box, poll books, certificates, etc., to the county clerk who unlocks the box in the presence of the election officers to see if the packages containing the ballots are properly sealed, and if so, the county clerk issues his receipt for the box and ballots—one to the judge, and one to the sheriff.

The county clerk within a certain time sends the ballots to a canvassing board which examines them and makes an official announcement of the number of votes cast for each candidate, and gives them a certificate of their election. The successful candidates are notified and later installed into office.

AMENDMENTS TO CONSTITUTION.

Amendments to the Constitution are handled in the same way as an election. The ballot contains the amendment proposed with "Yes" or "No" printed at the side. The party voting crosses out one of these words, puts the ballot in the blank envelope and returns it as in an election.

VOTING BY MAIL.

Voting by mail is often a great convenience.

The world is becoming more democratic and the right to vote for representation is now arranged so that all eligible citizens of the United States, twenty-one and over, may have a part in governing his or her country.

If a voter is out of the state or county and holds his residence in the same place as when he voted last—or calls home—he or she can vote by mail. He must first register, which is also done by mail.

A printed ballot with return envelope is sent to him. The ballot is marked by placing a cross opposite the name of the candidate voted for, then put in a blank envelope, sealed and enclosed in an envelope addressed to the secretary or clerk of the county or chairman of the tellers.

This envelope must be signed by the one voting. The blank envelope containing the ballot is opened and the ballot deposited in the ballot box.

The one voting must take an oath before a notary public that he or she is eligible.

ELECTORS FOR PRESIDENT AND VICE PRESIDENT.

When the voters go to the polls on election day to vote for President and Vice President every four years on the first Tuesday after the first Monday in November they really cast their ballots for the electors who were nominated at the state convention. The names of the state electors of each party are printed on the ballots under the party name. The ones receiving the most votes are elected, and are morally bound to vote for the candidate of the party that elected them.

The campaign continues until the election on the first Tuesday after the first Monday in November. The electors elected in November meet at their state capital in January and vote for President and Vice President. The result of this vote is dispatched at once to the President of the Senate at Washington, D. C. The electors of the different states meet at Washington on the morning of the second Monday in January after their election, and give their vote at or after twelve o'clock according to law.

On the second Wednesday in February succeeding the meeting of the electors, the Senate and House of Representatives meet in the Hall of Representatives at 1 o'clock p. m. with the President of the Senate presiding.

Two tellers are appointed in each House to whom shall be handed, as they are opened by the President of the Senate, all the certificates and papers purporting to be certificates of the —— electoral voters, which certificates and papers shall be opened, presented and acted upon in alphabetical order of the states; said tellers having then read the same in the presence and hearing of the two Houses, shall make a list of the voters as they shall appear from the said certificates, and the votes having been ascertained and counted, according to law; the result of the same shall be delivered to the President of the Senate, who shall announce the result of the vote, which announcement shall be deemed a sufficient declaration of the persons elected President and Vice President of the United States, and together with the list of voters be entered on the journals of the two Houses.

If no one receives a majority of all the electoral votes the Constitution provides that the House of Representatives shall choose a President and the Senate a Vice President. (Article XII, National Constitution.)

The President and Vice President are inaugurated on March 4th succeeding the election.

They take the oath of office on a platform on the east front of the Capitol. The President delivers an address outlining his policies, then returns to the White House.

nine

Taxation.

The national government is supported by taxation in various ways, and it requires a great amount of money to carry on the business of our country even in times of peace—over $2,000,000,000. This money is raised through a system of taxation of two kinds—direct and indirect.

A direct tax is a tax on real property or a poll tax.

An indirect tax is a tax on one individual, but is indirectly paid by another. (Taxes assessed on merchandise are indirect, as the consumer pays them.)

Most of the money is raised by import duties and excise taxes.

Import duties are taxes on imported goods.

Excise tax is a tax levied on goods manufactured in this country.

Duties are taxes on goods imported from foreign countries. The consumer on imported goods indirectly pays the duty assessed by the government.

There are two kinds of duties—specific and ad valorem.

Specific duties are fixed amounts levied on certain commodities as the yard, pound and gallon.

Ad valorem duties are levied at a certain rate per cent on the value of the articles taxed.

Duties are leviable on either imports or exports.

Imports relate only to goods brought into the country from abroad.

Exports relate to goods sent out of a country.

There is a special system for the collection of import duties, by naming many places along the coast to be used as "ports of entry," where custom houses in charge of collectors have been established. "Each custom house has a collector and the government has employed a large force of officers and special agents to overtake any dishonesty—attempting to smuggle goods through without paying duty."

The state legislature levies the state tax, the city council the city tax, and the taxes to keep up the national government are levied by Congress.

The law making power of Congress and state legislatures not only have the power of passing laws, raising money by taxation, but also the right and power of saying how that money shall be spent.

There are several kind of taxes collected for the benefit of the county, town, city and state, viz.: Poll tax, income, inheritance, franchise, property.

Poll tax: This is a tax on the person and not on property. A male citizen twenty-one and over must pay a poll tax of $1.00 even if he has no property. He must pay this tax before he can vote. In Kentucky the poll tax is one dollar.

Income Tax: There is an income tax levied on the income one receives and not on the amount of property he has. It is levied on salaries or profits upon business. Unmarried persons with an income of over $1,000.00 and married persons with an income of over $2,000.00 must pay an income tax.

Inheritance Tax: Many states have an inheritance tax levied on property inherited. This tax is really designated to reach wealthy people, and is easily collected since probate court records state the amounts. Kentucky has an inheritance tax, drawn and introduced by L. F. Johnson, of Frankfort, in 1906.

Franchise Tax: The government or state gives to a person or corporation special privileges, the rights to use the streets of a city for railway, water, lighting, gas plants, etc., is considered valuable property in the right vested in them by their franchise. This is really a source of income and should be taxed.

Property Tax: Property owners pay a large part of the money raised by taxation. Personal property which includes bonds, stocks, mortgages, household goods, jewels, etc.

Real estate which includes houses, lots, lands and building.

While taxes are levied upon real estate there are some kinds of property exempt from taxation, viz.: public institutions and libraries, cemeteries, school houses, churches, and other public buildings.

A great amount of revenue is derived by state and local governments from licenses, fees and special assessments. Men and women engaged in certain kinds of business must pay to the national, state and local governments a license or fees, as merchants, peddlers, manufacturers, pawnbrokers, etc.

A fee is a sum paid to an officer of the government, state, city or county for performing some public service or for a license in business. If you wanted to get a deed to land recorded you would have to pay the officer a fee.

The expense of our government is enormous, but the paying of taxes is one way in which all must take part.

ACQUISITION OF NEW TERRITORY.

While the acquisition of new territory has increased the expenses of our nation, yet it has made us the greatest nation in the world.

We have expanded by acquisition of new possessions which Congress organized under the direct control of the "Federal Government," but giving them limited powers of self government, through legislation of their own. When their population is sufficient they will be admitted as states.

Today our national flag contains forty-eight stars, and no part of the United States except Alaska and Hawaii remains under a territorial form of government.

Alaska was purchased from Russia in 1867.

The President of the United States, with the advice and consent of the Senate, appoints the governor and judges of the courts.

They have a legislature composed of two houses whose members are elected by the people. A delegate to Congress with the right to take part in debates but not to vote is also elected by the people.

Hawaii: Hawaii is a regularly organized territory and is governed like Alaska; President appointing the governor with the consent of the Senate, etc.

Possessions: The Philippines, Porto Rico, and other islands are possessions rather than territories of the United States.

Philippines: The Governor General and eight commissioners appointed by the President with the advice and consent of the Senate are at the head of the general government of the Philippines.

"Five members of the commission are heads of the executive departments as well as having legislative powers. The other four members have only legislative power."

Commission: The nine members of the commission appointed by the President constitute the Upper House of the Legislature known as the Senate.

Lower House: The members of the Lower House of Representatives are elected by the people of the various civilized districts.

The nine commissioners represent the legislative body and have control of that part of the island not civilized.

Courts: They have a system of courts in which the judges of the Supreme Court are appointed by the President, and the judges of the lower courts are appointed by the Governor General with the approval of the commission.

Commissioners: There are two resident commissioners sent to the United States from the Philippines with seats in the House of Representatives, but cannot vote, only taking part in the debates.

Provinces: The islands are divided into provinces "each of which is governed by a provincial board of three members, and each province has its own city or town with its local government." Two of the members of the boards are elected by the people, and the third, who is the treasurer, is appointed by the Governor General, but usually a "Filipino."

Porto Rico.

Under President Wilson's administration "The new organic law granted the people of Porto Rico a greater self government than they had ever enjoyed."

They have a Governor appointed by the President, a legislature of two Houses elected by the people, and a system of courts.

"There are seventy-six cities and towns which enjoy some local government."

They send as their representative to Congress, a resident commissioner. While these new possessions are expensive they add great wealth and power to our nation.

Taxes are contributions that the people are required by the government to pay in order to meet the expenses of our nation.

We are not patriotic unless we respond to the call of our government.

Referendum and Initiative.

Some states have the referendum and initiative power of helping to make laws.

If a state legislature passes a law that the people do not approve of a petition may be signed by a certain number of voters which will require the law to be referred to the people for their approval or disapproval.

Referendum means referring a law passed by the legislature back to the voters for their approval or disapproval.

"If five per cent of the voters of a state and two-thirds of the congressional districts do not approve of a bill passed by the General Assembly they sign a petition and file it with the Secretary of State in ninety days after the General Assembly adjourns." The question involved is then submitted to the voters at the next election for their approval or disapproval.

The initiative is the right of the voters to start legislation. The object of the initiative and the referendum is to compel legislative bodies to act and respect the will of the people whom they represent.

The initiative petition must be filed four months before the regular election with the Secretary of State.

THE DISTRICT OF COLUMBIA.

The District of Columbia, including Washington, the Capital of the United States, is governed by Congress and by judicial and executive officers appointed by the President of the United States. The people have no power of self government.

The Constitution gives Congress the exclusive right of government in the District of Columbia.

It is governed by three commissioners appointed by the President. One must be an officer of the army and the other two appointed from civil life.

Congress keeps a watch over the District, and devotes certain days to considering the business of the District.

The courts of the district are Court of Appeals, Supreme Court, police court, justices of the peace.

The judicial officers are appointed by the President.

The District of Columbia has no representative in Congress.

PANAMA CANAL ZONE.

The Panama Canal Zone is under the control of a governor who is appointed by the President of the United States.

"It is neutral and open to vessels of commerce and war of all nations, but war vessels must pass through without delay and while in the canal cannot load or unload troops or munitions of war."

The cost of the construction of the canal was about $400,000,000. It shortens the voyage from New York to San Francisco 8,000 miles.

Guam and Samoan Islands.

These islands are naval stations and are governed by the naval officers stationed there.

COMMERCE.

Commerce is divided between the state and Federal governments. We have interstate commerce, foreign commerce and commerce with the Indians. Congress regulates commerce.

Interstate commerce is carried on in the United States, as when goods are shipped from one state to another, or one place in a state to another, either by land or water. The Interstate Commerce Commission provided for by Congress is composed of nine men appointed by the President, and regulates interstate commerce. The members of this commission receive a salary of $10,000.00 annually.

Foreign Commerce.

Foreign commerce is commerce carried on with foreign countries. Certain regulations are prescribed for vessels engaged in foreign commerce, "Enter" and "Clear" ports.

All vessels registered in the United States are protected by the government in any part of the world. Only vessels can be registered by a citizen of the United States. No foreign vessel can register.

Congress regulates commerce with foreign nations and among the states, and Indian tribes.

Indian Tribes.

The government looks after the interest of "Indian affairs." There are about 300,000 Indians on 150 reservations in different states and territories all under the protection of the United States.

NATIONAL PARKS.

The national government has set aside several large tracts of land for National Parks. The Yellowstone National Park is about half as large as Massachusetts and is the most beautiful and interesting park in the world.

ten

Voter's Duty as a Citizen.

To vote is an expression of choice for this man or woman for an office. The ballot is the only efficient way to express public opinion and should be regarded as a sacred trust.

Every person in the state is either a citizen or alien.

"An alien is a person born in a foreign country who lives here, but is still a subject of some other country."

An alien may become a citizen of the United States after he has lived in this country for five years and in the state one year. He must be able to read and write his name, to speak English and be of moral character.

Only white persons and negroes may become naturalized.

"Chinese, Japanese and East Indians cannot become citizens unless born in the United States."

Unmarried women can become citizens like the men.

A married woman is a citizen if her husband is a citizen. She cannot become naturalized by herself. A woman born in the United States who marries an alien ceases to be an American citizen and becomes a subject of the country to which her husband belongs.

The wife of a man not a citizen of the United States cannot vote in this country.

If a resident of the United States she resumes her citizenship at the death of her husband, or if she is divorced.

A foreign born woman who marries a citizen becomes a citizen.

An American born may live abroad for many years and not lose his or her citizenship.

An alien enjoys the same protection of the law as does the citizen.

CITIZEN.

A citizen is a person born in the United States and subject to the jurisdiction thereof.

We are living in a democratic government which is a priceless heritage and a great blessing to mankind.

Democracy demands a sense of responsibility, personal interest in the affairs of government and respect for human rights.

As citizens we must become more conscious and appreciative of the inheritance our forefathers left us. This great inheritance is a wonderful land of opportunity and freedom.

To be an intelligent and desirable citizen we must have a knowledge of our Constitution, and know by whom and how our country is governed.

The man or woman who does not possess some knowledge of how the country is governed—as has been said—may easily become a prey of persons who are anxious to advance their own interests at the expense of the people.

The things needed for the use and protection of the people are provided by the people through their government.

As a part of the community you enjoy the good roads, streets, schools, libraries and many other things; therefore, you have no right to shirk your duty in not helping to maintain your government. If we enjoy the good things in this life without doing our part to have them we are cowards.

To live in a country and enjoy its freedom, peace and comforts and not do our part toward maintaining such peace and comforts we have failed to do our duty toward our fellowman and government, and may be called a sponger, a coward and a shirker if we fail to vote and do our part toward maintaining our government.

It is not only our duty to vote but we should study and understand public questions so that we can vote intelligently on the issues of the day. We should be interested in the ballot for it is one way in which public opinion may be expressed.

Every man or woman under the protection of our government should feel obligated to give his or her best to make our government one of high ideals.

Plato said: "Only that state is healthy and can thrive which unceasingly endeavors to help the individuals who constitute it."

The United States is both a democracy and a republic.

A democracy means a government by the people.

A republic is a democracy in which the people elect representatives to carry on the government for them.

UNITED STATES.

The United States is a great republic composed of more than 100,000,000 citizens under the protection of one flag with forty-eight stars which represent the forty-eight states of the union.

"A citizen might be termed a member of a large society called the United States."

Every man, woman and child is a member of this society, unless an alien, an idiot, or convicted of some infamous crime.

The members of this great society when they reach the age of twenty-one have a duty to perform which should be a sacred one. In this society citizenship is defined in the national Constitution in the fourteenth amendment. "All persons born or naturalized in the United States and subject to the jurisdiction thereof are citizens of the United States and of the state wherein they reside."

One of the first duties of a citizen is to vote. If we fail to vote we have no right to complain of the condition of affairs, and how our government is managed.

It is a privilege to be a citizen of this great country and a member of this great "society called the United States." It should be a greater privilege to cast our vote in every election and know we are doing our part to keep up the government.

There are four ways which we, as citizens, can help maintain our government:

"First: Vote at every election, read and be interested in public affairs.

"Second: Help to manage public affairs and be ready to hold an office, if you are the choice of the people.

"Third: Try to understand public questions, so you can vote intelligently and criticize justly.

"Fourth: Remember to pay your share of the expense of doing the work."

There are now over 27,011,330 voting women in the United States, soon to take part in all elections, and share the responsibility as well as the privilege of suffrage.

In maintaining this great government of ours two parties are necessary to keep the wheels moving. As has been said, the two dominant parties now in existence are the Democratic party and Republican party.

We have learned that parties are means of securing united action among the voters who think alike. It was Washington who said: "The spirit of party unfortunately is inseparable from our nature, having its root in the strongest passions of the human mind."

There must be organization under the direction of leaders to secure united action.

Let the women of our country come forward and identify themselves with the party of their choice and organize under competent leaders, showing to the world we not only deem it a great privilege to vote, but are willing to share the responsibility of making our government the best in the world.

Will you do your bit to keep this great machinery moving onward and upward?

eleven

Why Should Women Vote?

It is important that every woman who possesses the constitutional and statutory qualifications should exercise her right to vote; because it is only in this way that there can be a fair expression of the political sentiment of the qualified voters on any question.

Another reason is that the right to vote is not only a privilege but a duty that is imposed by law, and where one is entitled to exercise that privilege, the failure to so exercise it is a failure to perform a duty on the part of the voter.

Then, if only a small per cent of the women were to vote, and a large per cent of the men were to vote, it would always be problematical as to what effect the consensus of the women's opinion would have had in the result, if a full vote had been polled; and this questionable result of an election is one of the dangers incident to the exercise of the right of suffrage. If the women manifest anything approaching a unanimous desire to participate in the exercise of this governmental function, it will have the effect to increase the public confidence in this government and its institutions.

Men and women without regard to race, color or social condition, must take their turn exactly alike at the polling place. Each ballot has exactly the same weight in the election, and the ballot of the poorest man counts just as much as the ballot of the most influential citizen. The voting place is the leveling place, and when women realize that the exercise of suffrage gives not only the equal right to vote, but also allows equal expression of opinion, then the better purpose of woman suffrage will have been accomplished. This equality is not a condescension on the part of women, but it is the exercise of a right under the law, to call for the fair expression of opinion from all the people of every social and political standard, without reference to mental ability, social standing or business prominence. Therefore, it is the duty of every intelligent woman to vote and use her influence to get the women interested in voting and doing their part in keeping up the government. We know that the lower classes will all vote and many floaters will be found in such classes, so it behooves the intelligent women to do their part. The vote is the equal right of every one who is qualified under the law, and every qualified person has one vote, and that one vote from each one is the thing which the Constitution is most zealous to secure and safeguard.

We appeal to every intelligent woman of the United States and especially in Kentucky to take part in the coming campaign. Organize under competent leaders and let your organization extend into every precinct. See that the voters register on the first Tuesday in October, or the special registration days, then on 2nd day of November go to the polls and vote for President and Vice President of the United States.

Women as well as men in Kentucky can vote for President and Vice President if twenty-one years old and over, unless an alien, idiot or have committed some infamous crime. We have suffrage so far, whether we want it or not, and let us, as intelligent women, not forget the duty it carries with it. We love our government and the good things it gives, as schools, good roads, protection of life and property and the many other things. Should we not be willing to do our part to get these things, or must we be a sponger, a coward, or shirker and let our fellow man do all? Should we fail to vote and help maintain our government we certainly will come under one of these heads, that is if we are able to go to the polls and register and vote, and fail to do it. If you are absent from the county or state you can vote by mail. There is no way to escape our duty unless providentially hindered.

]In Kentucky there are 1,201,185 voters, of which 663,454 are men and 537,731 are women. The white female voters are 477,731. The negro female voters are 60,000.

There are 13,225 foreign born white males of voting age, that have been naturalized.

Let us train ourselves for good citizenship and serve our nation, state, county, city and town in every way possible to make our government one of high ideals and the best in the world.

www.ingramcontent.com/pod-product-compliance
Lightning Source LLC
Chambersburg PA
CBHW032118280326
41933CB00009B/888